# Evaluate Yourself
## Personality

## *Other books in the series*

| | |
|---|---|
| Teenagers | Business |
| Sex | Brain Power |
| Psychology | Self-Improvement |
| Marriage | Personality |

## *Quiz-Master*

| | |
|---|---|
| Computers | Literature |
| Electronics | History |
| Mathematics | Economics |
| Physics | Travel |
| Environment | Hinduism |
| Plants | Wildlife |
| Sports | Media |
| Politics | Challenge |

## *Of allied interest*

Brain Teasers
Intelligence Tests

# Evaluate Yourself
## Personality

*(Professional guidance that will help you
to be poised and self-assured)*

*Contributors*
**Jane Sherrod Singer**
**Roz Ashley**

*Compiled and Edited by*
**Vijaya Kumar**

A Sterling Paperback

STERLING PAPERBACKS
An imprint of
Sterling Publishers (P) Ltd.
A-59, Okhla Industrial Area, Phase-II,
New Delhi-110020.
Tel: 26387070, 26386165; Fax: 91-11-26383788
E-mail: info@sterlingpublishers.com
www.sterlingpublishers.com

*Evaluate Yourself: Personality*
© 1998, Sterling Publishers (P) Ltd.
ISBN 978- 81 207 1984 2
Originally Published under the title: *Let's get Quizzical, Personality*
Reprint 2009

Quiz Material – Courtesy, Singer Media Corporation, California

All rights are reserved. No part of this publication
may be reproduced, stored in a retrieval system or transmitted,
in any form or by any means, mechanical, photocopying,
recording or otherwise, without prior written permission
of the original publishers.

*Published by* Sterling Publishers (P) Ltd., New Delhi-110020.
*Printed at* Sterling Publishers Pvt. Ltd., New Delhi-110020.

# Editor's Word

Personality is a term with many connotations. Sometimes, the word refers to the ability to get along well socially, sometimes it refers to the most striking impression that one makes on others. It deals with complex human behaviour including emotions, thought processes and actions. This quiz book reveals your personality traits and helps you to know yourself.

# Contents

|     | Editor's Word | v |
| --- | --- | --- |
| 1.  | Are you a good judge of human nature? | 1 |
| 2.  | How well do you live with yourself? | 5 |
| 3.  | What's your popularity rating? | 8 |
| 4.  | What kind of a person are you? | 11 |
| 5.  | Discover your personality | 15 |
| 6.  | Are you really a nice person? | 18 |
| 7.  | Are you an "in" person? | 21 |
| 8.  | Do you know how others see you? | 25 |
| 9.  | Do people really like you? | 29 |
| 10. | Are you friendly? | 33 |
| 11. | Are you easy to live with? | 36 |
| 12. | How carefree are you? | 40 |
| 13. | How poised are you? | 44 |
| 14. | How cordial are you? | 48 |
| 15. | Are you sensuous? | 51 |
| 16. | Are you an interesting person? | 55 |
| 17. | Are you a peaceful person? | 58 |
| 18. | Are you a pushover? | 61 |
| 19. | Do you have charm? | 68 |
| 20. | Do you talk too much? | 71 |
| 21. | Are you young in spirit? | 74 |

| | | |
|---|---|---|
| 22. | Are you young at heart? | 77 |
| 23. | Do you feel inferior? | 80 |
| 24. | How tacky are you? | 83 |
| 25. | Do you maintain your self-respect? | 87 |
| 26. | Are you in full command of your status symbols? | 90 |
| 27. | Can you make others happy? | 93 |
| 28. | Do you know the real you? | 96 |
| 29. | Do you irritate others? | 100 |
| 30. | How vulnerable are you? | 104 |
| 31. | Are you stubborn? | 108 |
| 32. | How imaginative are you? | 112 |
| 33. | Do you try too hard to be popular? | 116 |

# Are You A Good Judge Of Human Nature?

> *Many people who do poorly on information tests are particularly adept when it comes to understanding human nature—and many so-called "geniuses" are inept in matters of practical philosophy. The following test will reveal your ability to judge human nature.*

Tick one of the columns to indicate whether you feel that the statement is True or False.

|  | True | False |
|---|---|---|
| 1. It is unreasonable to expect human beings to be reasonable. | ☐ | ☐ |
| 2. The best way to succeed in business is to mix with influential people. | ☐ | ☐ |
| 3. The person who demands a great deal from other people usually gets a lot more than the person who is more polite. | ☐ | ☐ |
| 4. People of great ability are invariably vain and egotistical. | ☐ | ☐ |
| 5. Conversation is a device often used to conceal thought. | ☐ | ☐ |
| 6. If you do something well, people will surely and invariably recognise it and reward you. | ☐ | ☐ |
| 7. As people grow older, they become wiser and learn more. | ☐ | ☐ |
| 8. Things may be said with a smile that would cause violent quarrels if said without a smile. | ☐ | ☐ |
| 9. "What you can get by with" is a pretty good moral standard. | ☐ | ☐ |
| 10. You can do a welcome service to friends by telling them their shortcomings. | ☐ | ☐ |
| 11. A debtor naturally and invariably has a kindly feeling toward the |  |  |

|     |     | True | False |
|-----|-----|------|-------|
|     | person who has lent him or her money. | ☐ | ☐ |
| 12. | Nobody can absolutely understand another person. | ☐ | ☐ |
| 13. | When you give people more responsible jobs, they tend to develop more respect for authority. | ☐ | ☐ |
| 14. | People rejoice to hear their acquaintances praised. | ☐ | ☐ |
| 15. | Children who have loving parents separate from them more easily than children who were rejected by their parents. | ☐ | ☐ |
| 16. | A strong person makes more enemies than a weak person. | ☐ | ☐ |
| 17. | Highly intelligent men tend to marry brainless women. | ☐ | ☐ |
| 18. | A romantic person sees the real soul of the person he loves. | ☐ | ☐ |
| 19. | Given enough leisure and money, people would invariably read more, cultivate themselves more and do more worthwhile things. | ☐ | ☐ |
| 20. | Most people are unable to reason logically. | ☐ | ☐ |
| 21. | Just because you sometimes feel hatred toward someone, it does not mean you do not really love that person. | ☐ | ☐ |
| 22. | Most people fear everything that is new. | ☐ | ☐ |
| 23. | One can buy anything with money. | ☐ | ☐ |
| 24. | Business is corrupt and dishonest. | ☐ | ☐ |
| 25. | Women are more conservative than men. | ☐ | ☐ |

ANSWERS

Are you a good judge of human nature?

An argument can be made against almost every one of these answers, but let us assume that the answer indicates the statement is *generally* true or false.

| | | | |
|---|---|---|---|
| 1. True | 8. True | 15. True | 22. True |
| 2. False | 9. False | 16. False | 23. False |
| 3. False | 10. False | 17. False | 24. False |
| 4. False | 11. False | 18. False | 25. False |
| 5. True | 12. True | 19. False | |
| 6. False | 13. True | 20. True | |
| 7. False | 14. False | 21. True | |

Count up the number of correct answers and multiply by four. The result is your "Wisdom Percentage".

A percentage over 80 indicates you are a regular Solomon.

A score from 60 to 70 is about average.

A percentage less than 40 suggests that you should pay more attention to your own and other people's behaviour.

# ② How Well Do You Live With Yourself?

> *Most of us like to be around people, to share our joys and sorrows with them. But that is not always possible. Often one must fall back on his or her inner resources. Here are some questions about your own independence.*

**Indicate your answer by ticking one of the columns next to each question.**

|  | Yes | No |
|---|---|---|
| 1. Does the thought of spending an evening or afternoon alone throw you into a panic? | ☐ | ☐ |
| 2. When you are alone, do you find yourself constantly craving something to eat or drink? | ☐ | ☐ |
| 3. Do you have one or more hobbies that you can do alone? | ☐ | ☐ |
| 4. When you are bored or faced with unpleasantness, do you tend to go to sleep? | ☐ | ☐ |
| 5. Do you sometimes deliberately plan a time when you can be by yourself? | ☐ | ☐ |
| 6. Do you often find yourself telephoning people for no reason? | ☐ | ☐ |
| 7. Have you ever written a story or poem that you liked, even if you never showed it to anyone? | ☐ | ☐ |
| 8. Do you usually like your job, home, school, or work? | ☐ | ☐ |
| 9. When you take a trip or go shopping, are you unhappy unless someone is with you? | ☐ | ☐ |
| 10. Do you keep the volume of your radio or television turned up loud? | ☐ | ☐ |

Give yourself one point for each correct answer.

1. No
2. No
3. Yes
4. No
5. Yes
6. No
7. Yes
8. Yes
9. No
10. No

## Score

**Over 8 points:** You are self-reliant and live with yourself well. If you have missed question 8, however, you may be withdrawing too much from those around you.

**5-7 points:** You are, generally speaking, content with your own company. It may be force of habit that makes you feel lonely when no one is around. If you have not answered question 3 correctly, that may be the answer to your problem.

**2-4 points:** You are restless and get most of your inner strength from others. While you would probably do well in any work that brings you in contact with many people it would also be wise if you learn more about the joys of solitude.

**Less than 2 points:** You like to get lost in the noise and excitement of anything, any place — as long as you are not alone! Try spending a few minutes each day by yourself, lost in a book, a letter, a hobby. Increase the time in a week and soon you will find how nice it is to live with yourself.

# What's Your Popularity Rating?

**3**

> *To try too hard to be popular is often disastrous, but to meet those around you with warmth, concern and generosity can build real popularity. This test will show how you rate with those with whom you have contact.*

**Choose any one options.**
1. Do you ever take a dislike to a person at first sight?
   A. Often _____ B. Sometimes _____ C. Never _____
2. If a stranger begins a conversation with you do you ignore him/her?
   A. Often _____ B. Sometimes _____ C. Never _____
3. When someone tells you something in strict confidence, can you keep the information to yourself?
   A. Often _____ B. Sometimes _____ C. Never _____
4. Do people come to you to seek help or advice?
   A. Often _____ B. Sometimes _____ C. Never _____
5. When talking with others, do you refuse to listen to their topics and turn the stream of conversation to matters which are primarily concerned with your own interests?
   A. Often _____ B. Sometimes _____ C. Never _____
6. Do you use a tone of voice in conversation which is critical, sarcastic or aggressive?
   A. Often _____ B. Sometimes _____ C. Never _____
7. When something you yourself have done goes wrong, do you try to place the blame on someone else?
   A. Often _____ B. Sometimes _____ C. Never _____
8. When a new neighbour or worker moves in or joins your group do you take it upon yourself to make the first advances of friendship?
   A. Often _____ B. Sometimes _____ C. Never _____

9. In cases of emergency to others, when your assistance is urgently needed, do you unhesitatingly drop your own job, chores and interests to help out?
A. Often ____ B. Sometimes ____ C. Never ____

### ANSWERS
1. a-0; B-10; C-5
2. A-0; B-10; C-0
3. A-10; B-0; C-0
4. A-10; B-5; C-0
5. A-0; B-5; C-10
6. A-0; B-5; C-10
7. A-0; B-5; C-10
8. A-10; B-5; C-0
9. A-10; B-5; C-0

### YOUR SCORE
**70-90:** This is an exceptionally high score. If you answered honestly, you regard values and people, who find you reliable. You do not go out of your way for acclaim but your actions bring it to you.

**45-65:** Testees in this bracket are usually helped when they widen their interests. They want to be liked but are often business-bound or house-bound.

**0-40:** People in this bracket are usually so shy that they fear popularity. Once they break out of their shell they are the most popular people around.

# What Kind Of A Person Are You? ④

> *Your home, surroundings, cherished possessions, the things you want and your use of leisure time are indications of the real you. Try to disregard your present environment, whether you are pleased with it or not. If you dream—perhaps, the impossible dream—what items would you check in the following quiz as being the nearest to your wishes today?*

**Tick your choice.**
1. I would like to live in:
   a. A bungalow with picture windows and a broad roof.
   b. A sleek house of ultra-modern design.
   c. A farm house.
   d. An apartment.
2. My living room would look out upon:
   a. The ocean.
   b. A garden or fields.
   c. A hand-wrought iron gate and high wall.
   d. A gushing fountain.
3. I would like to own:
   a. A sports car.
   b. An antique car which runs well.
   c. A new station wagon.
   d. A two-door coupe.
4. I would choose a vacation:
   a. On a luxury cruise to some far-off land.
   b. At the best hotel in the biggest city.
   c. Roughing it out in some remote spot.
   d. At home, doing as I please.
5. My closet would primarily contain:
   a. Formal clothing.
   b. Casualwear.
   c. Woollens.
   d. A mixture of everything, ranging from old worn-out favourites to evening clothing.

ANSWERS

Check the choices you made in the test with the descriptions given below. If 3 or more descriptions are generally similar, you can assume this is the type of person you are.
1. Your choice of living quarters:
    a. A bungalow with large windows suggests that you are interested in knowing people. The broad roof suggests a God-fearing person.
    b. An ultra-modern home is usually selected by well-organised, sophisticated people.
    c. A farm house indicates a romantic nature. You probably like open space and nature.
    d. Your choice of an apartment indicates a businesslike mind. You dislike trivial details and can relegate responsibilities to others.
2. Your choice of view:
    a. On ocean view suggests a restless, unfilled type of personality, but one with great dreams.
    b. A flower garden or fields is usually selected by a home-lover and/or a person with infinite patience and inner tranquillity.
    c. High walls and ornate fences are for people who have no desire to meet others. Usually they are aloof, self-contained or fearful.
    d. A gushing fountain indicates an outgoing personality, the type of person who is fresh, eager and usually laughs often.
3. Your choice of cars:
    a. A sports car hints that you want to be on the go but are not particularly interested in where. You like attention.
    b. Antique cars are, like farm houses, a sign of a romantic person. This type of personality may be conservative and conventional.

    c. A new station wagon is usually selected by people who love large families, have many friends and are home-bodies.

    d. A two-door coupe is for the shy person, a little fearful of places, people and things.

4. Your choice of a vacation:

    a. If you wish a luxury cruise to some far-off place you are showing escapist qualities—a dreamer. You have a love of beauty and tend to dress exotically.

    b. A choice of the best hotel is a hint that you are a social climber or are looking for a rich mate. If married, you are weary of your home life.

    c. The desire to rough it out indicates that, at heart, you are an individualist and feel cramped by your present surroundings and by too many people.

    d. If you wish to stay at home, you are practical, self-satisfied and self-contained—perhaps even in a rut.

5. Your choice of clothing:

    a. You are impractical and romantic, harbouring ideas of grandeur. Very likely you are discontented with life.

    b. This type of wardrobe is selected by the outdoor, active type. You are probably outgoing, likeable and pleasant to be with.

    c. Woollens are the choice of fastidious people who are well-organised and unemotional.

    d. A mixture of clothing is usually found in the closets of well-adapted people who can fit into almost any circumstance.

# Discover Your Personality

|5|

> *Some personalities seem to fit into the pattern of life with greater ease than others. But difficult personalities can be changed, shaped and polished for the better—provided the person really wishes to improve himself. This is designed to clue you about yourself. It can be your starting point for self-improvement. Remember no one is so perfect that he cannot become a better human being.*

Below is a list of 40 adjectives and phrases. Check 12 of them which you think best describe your personality.

| | | | |
|---|---|---|---|
| 1. | self-controlled | 2. | slow |
| 3. | creative | 4. | easily bored |
| 5. | peaceful | 6. | evasive |
| 7. | modest | 8. | lazy |
| 9. | logical | 10. | cynical |
| 11. | inquisitive | 12. | untidy |
| 13. | sympathetic | 14. | stubborn |
| 15. | prompt | 16. | self-centred |
| 17. | consistent | 18. | always serious |
| 19. | adaptable | 20. | fickle |
| 21. | helpful | 22. | a scoffer |
| 23. | outgoing | 24. | easily hurt |
| 25. | tactful | 26. | emotional |
| 27. | love of beauty | 28. | fearful |
| 29. | alert | 30. | unimaginative |
| 31. | reverent | 32. | indecisive |
| 33. | dependable | 34. | critical |
| 35. | truthful | 36. | belligerent |
| 37. | sense of humour | 38. | introverted |
| 39. | hardworking | 40. | conceited |

ANSWERS

1. If your list of 12 adjectives and phrases includes 8 odd-numbered and 4 even-numbered selections, you are a normal, well-adjusted person who is honest.
2. If you checked more than 4 even numbers, the chances are that your personality can stand

improvement since these reactions are overwhelmingly negative.
3. If your answers include more than 8 odd-numbered selections you are probably an egotist. You, too, have personality traits which can be corrected.

# Are You Really A Nice Person? ⑥

> *No one likes a "know-it-all", but be sure that you aren't one yourself... or at least have some of the failings. Perhaps this will give you some clues.*

**Choose any one option.**
1. A friend is telling a story but errs on some unimportant details. You would:
   a. let the small errors pass.
   b. interrupt and correct your friend.
   c. correct him when he is finished.
2. You are served some unfamiliar food which you do not like. You would:
   a. try your best to eat it.
   b. tell about the cooking you like best.
   c. push your plate back and order something else.
3. A friend appears wearing a new coat you have seen on sale. You would:
   a. mention the sale.
   b. say nothing.
   c. make a complimentary comment about the garment.
4. A neighbour has spent his vacation at home, but you have had an extensive trip. You would:
   a. tell him every detail of your trip.
   b. answer any questions he asks about your vacation.
   c. tell him that he hasn't really lived.
5. You have just read a review of a current best-selling book. A friend asks you if you have read it. You would:
   a. say that you have not read the book.
   b. say you have any quote points from the review.
   c. say you have only read the review.

6. Among your relatives, there is one very famous person. You would:
   a. mention his name whenever possible.
   b. talk about his bad points.
   c. express modest pride when his name is mentioned.
7. You have a hobby or talent in which you excel. You would:
   a. express a disregard for the hobbies of others.
   b. keep your secret techniques to yourself.
   c. teach others who express a desire to learn.
8. You are shown a rare plant. You would:
   a. say you don't think much of it.
   b. say you have seen dozens that are more interesting.
   c. ask questions about it.

DESIRABLE REACTIONS

| | | |
|---|---|---|
| 1-a | 2-a | 3-c |
| 4-b | 5-c | 6-c |
| 7-c | 8-c. | |

SCORING

**7 to 8 correct:** You are sensitive to the feeling of others and never push yourself in the limelight. Because of this, you are genuinely well-liked and never criticised for being a Know-It-All.

**3 to 6 correct:** You are very self-centred and prone to talk too much about yourself, and your achievements. People often are uncomfortable with you and shake their heads when you leave. Watch Out!

**0 to 2 correct:** "They always talk who never think." (Prior)

# Are You An "In" Person? ⑦

> *Everyone wants to have friends and to be liked. Each individual wishes to be "in" the group, large or small. Those who claim that these statements are incorrect merely kid themselves.*
>
> *The art of making friends, of being accepted, of being comfortable among others can be cultivated. Using this test as a beginning point, on which step of the ladder are you?*

**In the following situations, which reaction is nearest to your own?**
1. When travelling alone, you usually
   a. read.
   b. talk to those around you.
   c. study people.
2. You can name
   a. 3 or more *real* friends.
   b. 1 or 2 *real* friends.
   c. no friends but many acquaintances.
3. If you attend a party and know only the host or hostess, you would
   a. stay close to those who are giving the party.
   b. be happy to have been invited.
   c. worry about your intrusion.
   d. leave at the earliest possibility.
4. If you were to enter a crowded, informal cafeteria or lunchroom at noon and find only one chair available at a table where others are eating, you would
   a. wait until a table is ready.
   b. leave.
   c. ask if you may join the diners and take the empty chair.
5. At a dinner party surrounded by unfamiliar faces, if you wished another helping of a dish, you would
   a. say nothing.
   b. help yourself.
   c. compliment your hostess and ask for another helping.

6. You find that you have selected the wrong attire for a social gathering. You would
   a. withdraw to a corner.
   b. try to act as you always do.
   c. make a big joke of it.
7. At a lecture with a large audience in attendance, you feel keenly opposed to a statement which is made. You would
   a. speak up.
   b. gulp down your thoughts.
   c. make your point after someone else has "broken the ice".
8. During a two-week vacation at a resort, you usually
   a. remain alone.
   b. make friends and plan things to do together.
   c. find a couple of people and spend time with them.
9. If you were dancing and the music suddenly changed from a sweet, loving tune to a hot Go-go or vice versa, you would
   a. leave the floor.
   b. enter happily into the change of pace even if you do not know the dance steps.
   c. be embarrassed but struggle along.

### ADD YOUR SCORE BY POINTS
1. a-5; b-0; c-3
2. a-0; b-2; c-15
3. a-3; b-0; c-10; d-15
4. a-10; b-15; c-0
5. a-10; b-15; c-0
6. a-15; b-0; c-4
7. a-0; b-15; c-3
8. a-15; b-0; c-5
9. a-15; b-0; c-4

## ANALYSIS

**75-125:** You are not "in" with groups but "inside" yourself. There are times when you bluster but basically you are shy. However, you probably feel lonely at times and want to make contact with people. To be "in" with people, one has to get "out" of one's emotional shell.

**30-74:** This is an average range. You pick and choose your time, your place and the things you want to do. You are friendly, charming, intelligent and discriminating.

**0-29:** You can make friends any place, anytime. You are gregarious to the point of being offensive, sometimes to the more introspective members of the group around you. This is a rousing good score for an "in" personality and the chances are that you have the world on a string.

# 8

## Do You Know How Others See You?

> *The word "image" is very popular these days. Politicians work fiendishly to create a desirable "image". Actors and actresses watch how they dress and act so that their "image" will or will not change. Psychiatrists refer to "father" and "mother" images. And most employees want a favourable "image" in the minds of their bosses. Most of us think we know ourselves, but sometimes during periods of self-evaluation, we pause to wonder how others see us. This test will help you see yourself through the eyes of others.*

**Check the one most typical of your behaviour.**
1. When you laugh, is it usually
   a. rather robust and hearty?
   b. more of a smile and a chuckle than a laugh?
   c. a subdued, almost private laugh?
   d. a bit brittle or cynical?
   e. deep-throated, slightly suggestive?
2. In bed at night, as you begin to sleep, do you lie
   a. stretched out on your back?
   b. stretched out on your stomach?
   c. with your head cradled on one of your arms?
   d. curled up?
   e. with your head almost or completely covered under the bedclothes?
3. When you sit down to relax for any length of time, for instance to read or watch television, which posture do you usually adopt?
   a. fairly upright with legs and feet together
   b. one leg bent and tucked under you
   c. knees together but feet several inches apart
   d. legs crossed or twined one around the other
   e. legs straight out with feet crossed at the ankles
4. When sitting and talking with friends, do you
   a. have a habit of touching or prodding the person with whom you are talking?
   b. sit fairly still with your hands clasped?
   c. tug at your ear, pull your hair, stroke your chin or in some other way often touch your face with your hand?
   d. play with a cigarette, a ring, keys or anything else that is handy?

  e. adjust your clothing, such as pull down your skirt, straighten your tie, tuck in your sari, crease your trousers?
5. When walking, do you usually
  a. take long striding steps with your head high?
  b. take fairly short, stabbing steps?
  c. have loose hip movements rocking from side to side?
  d. look at the ground most of the time?
  e. walk with a swing, using your arms and legs loosely.

### SCORING

Look at your selections of answers for the questions. In all probability you have checked the same key-letter, a, b, c, d, or e, several times. If the same letter has been checked four or five times, your personality type is quite definite. If the same letter comes up three times, it is still evidence of a strong characteristic. If your selections are scattered, the analysis is given later.

### ANALYSIS

**The "A" Personality:** You are confident, forthright and ambitious. You dislike playing second fiddle and want to be the one who runs things. It could be that you are overly dominant, possessive, outspoken and even quick-tempered. You frighten some people, but those who know you well respect your drive and ability.

**The "B" Personality:** The selection of four or more B's indicates a sane and sensible person—down-to-earth, methodical and practical. You probably dislike change and hesitate to experiment too extravagantly.

**The "C" Personality:** You are very likely the sensitive, sympathetic, artistic type. You like people and have a need for them to like you. You can be temperamental, impatient and moody. The "C" personality tends to be generous and impulsive. They are wonderful friends but can be easily misused by those who pretend respect or love.

**The "D" Personality:** Shyness and insecurity are your major characteristics. Although you want people to like you, you will not relax enough to let them get to you. In all probability you worry unnecessarily, fret about small things. However, because of your shyness, you are more of a listened than a talker. Therefore, you have a vast fund of information and feelings stored away which will serve you well if you utilise it correctly.

**The "E" Personality:** You are not too far apart from the "A" personality except that you are probably more vain, restless and self-centred. While the "A" personality is a "go-getter" you are more relaxed and secure in your ambitions. In general, you expect people to come to you. You want a cat to jump on your lap, the dog to lie at your feet. People admire you for this assurance but can sometimes be over-awed.

**The "A-B-C-D-E" Personality:** This scattered selection is quite normal. You could be a mixture of caution with an artistic sensitivity and shy under new situations, as an example. People tend to like you because they can never be quite sure what your reactions will be. Therefore, you may be a headache but you'll never be a bore.

# Do People Really Like You? ⑨

> *With a very few neurotic exceptions, everyone wants to be accepted and liked. Indeed, some pay a high price to appear popular—from trying to buy friendships with money to the misuse of sex to gain attention. The real test is the everyday behaviour of those around you and the friends you find during an emergency. The following will help you assess whether or not people really like you.*

**Pick your choice.**
1. When you are ill
   a. Many people call or send cards.
   b. You sit it out pretty much alone.
   c. Several of your best friends check in.
2. When you meet a crowd of friends
   a. All of them say hello.
   b. Most keep on with their conversations.
   c. Some greet you more enthusiastically than others.
3. People you know
   a. Seem to go out of their way to be nice to you.
   b. Are preoccupied with their own lives.
   c. See you when it is convenient.
4. If you are short of money
   a. Many people are there to help you.
   b. Everyone else is broke too.
   c. There is always someone you can depend on.
5. When you have a birthday
   a. Many people remember the date.
   b. You have to hint for cards and presents.
   c. Some old standbys never forget.
6. People come to you for advice or help
   a. Often.
   b. Seldom or never.
   c. When you happen to be there.
7. You can honestly say
   a. "I like most people, regardless of race or creed."
   b. "I feel estranged from many people."
   c. "I am highly selective of my friends."

8. If you were asked to help in an important community drive, you would
   a. 'Make' the time to participate.
   b. Beg off for some reason.
   c. Work a little to show your approval.
9. When you return from a vacation
   a. People call and come to welcome you home.
   b. No one seems to notice that you were away.
   c. You call friends to tell them you are back.
10. You are elected to hold offices in clubs
    a. Many times.
    b. Never.
    c. Once or twice.
11. You are
    a. Occasionally the brunt of a joke.
    b. Often teased.
    c. A self-effacing clown.
12. When with older or younger people, you
    a. Find their conversation genuinely interesting.
    b. Are bored.
    c. Try to look interested even if you are not.
13. Generally speaking, you
    a. Try to solve your own problems.
    b. Go to many people with your tales of woe.
    c. Confide in those close to you.

**ANSWERS**
Give yourself 3 points for each A answer; 1 point for each B answer; 2 points for each C answer.

**YOUR SCORE**
**30-39:** Yes. People like you very much. You obviously have the quality of winning friendship and respect. It could be that you sometimes become weary of so much attention and applause, of being asked to do everything at all times. For your own sake, you must occasionally relax and let your host of friends take over.

**20-29:** You are probably thought of as reliable and likeable. This is a high score and one which is normally rated by good members of a community with a wholesome family life. You have few friendship problems.

**10-19:** You have a few very good friends. "The friends thou hast, grapple to thy soul with hooks of steel" (Shakespeare). It might also be wise to expand your list of friends.

**0-9:** The score of a lonely person. The approval of others can only be gained by your trust in them. You must make the first step, give the handshake. You will be surprised what will happen!

# Are You Friendly?

**10**

> *There are very few of us who have not wondered at one time or another if people really like us. Or are they just being polite? Or is there some other motive behind their friendliness? Then too, everyone wants to be liked and accepted. If you are one of those who have trouble making friends, perhaps, this quiz will help. Anyhow, let's just take it for fun!*

**Answer Yes or No.**

|  | Yes | No |
|---|---|---|
| 1. Do you like most people? | ☐ | ☐ |
| 2. Do you always have a compliment to give—even if you don't mean it? | ☐ | ☐ |
| 3. Do you enjoy listening to other people? | ☐ | ☐ |
| 4. Do you entertain others, even when you can't afford to? | ☐ | ☐ |
| 5. Is it relatively easy for you to admit an error and apologise? | ☐ | ☐ |
| 6. Do you join social clubs and/or groups which give you the feeling of being important? | ☐ | ☐ |
| 7. When giving gifts, do you present them as quietly and unobtrusively as possible? | ☐ | ☐ |
| 8. Are your work and social schedules so full that you must often turn people down in emergencies? | ☐ | ☐ |
| 9. Would you rather go without something you want than borrow it (or the money to get it)? | ☐ | ☐ |
| 10. Are you more considerate of people you consider to be your superiors that to others? | ☐ | ☐ |
| 11. Are *real* emergencies the only things that make you late or cause you to break dates, cancel appointments or be tardy? | ☐ | ☐ |
| 12. Are most of your friends of the same sex? | ☐ | ☐ |

|  | Yes | No |
|---|---|---|
| 13. Are you usually happy and "at home with yourself" when you are alone? | ☐ | ☐ |

## Scoring

Give yourself one point for each ODD numbered question which you have answered with Yes. (Desirably, the even numbered questions should be answered No, but we'll just consider questions 1, 3, 5, 7, etc.)

## Rating

**7 correct answers:** You have no trouble acquiring a friend. You're thoughtful, considerate, and seldom offend.

**4 to 6 correct answers:** Do people really like you? We say they do. Not everyone you meet—but really quite a few.

**1 to 3 correct answers:** Polish up your manners; put others yourself, or you'll find your life is empty and you're sitting on the shelf.

**0 correct answer:** 0 says no answer right. This makes us very sad. Friends are always earned and kept. They're not a passing fad.

It takes a lot of trying, a lot of thinking too... But it's really worth the effort when people really like you!

# Are You Easy To Live With?

⑪

> *Of course you are—or are you? Unless you are a loner, you love or work with others. Togetherness brings about the need for wholesome, well-defined respect for your colleagues or partner or family members. These questions will reveal the truth if you answer them honestly!*

**Select one from each.**
1. When the alarm-clock rings in the morning, do you
   a) Turn over for a few more minutes?
   b) Rise and shine?
   c) Stay in bed until the last possible moment?
2. Do you appear at breakfast
   a) All spruced up?
   b) Dressed, but not ready to go out?
   c) Dishevelled and in your dressing-gown?
3. On most mornings, are you
   a) Anxious to keep to your usual routine?
   b) Always half-asleep?
   c) Reluctant to start the day?
4. You meet your husband (or wife) for a restaurant lunch. Are you
   a) Full of the morning's woes?
   b) Anxious to make the occasion especially pleasant?
   c) Your normal self?
5. You're watching your favourite TV programme when a friend of your husband (or wife) calls and wants to talk. Do you
   a) Switch off without a word?
   b) Turn down the sound but continue viewing?
   c) Suggest that the visitor looks in too?
6. Do you think your husband (or wife):
   a) Good at heart but a bit tiresome?
   b) A wonderful person to live with?
   c) Just an ordinary person?

7. Do you
   a) Always remember birthdays and other anniversaries?
   b) Consider such sentimentality childish, even though conventionally marking the occasion?
   c) Forget them as often as not?
8. Do you direct attention to your partner's faults in front of your children
   a) Never?
   b) Sometimes?
   c) Regularly?
9. Which do you consider the most annoying
   a) Being late for meals?
   b) Being a poor shopper?
   c) Being absent-minded?
10. Do you consider the need for occasional solitude among married folk
    a) An unhealthy sign?
    b) Probably beneficial?
    c) Just a fad?
11. Do you discuss other people:
    a) Critically?
    b) Humorously?
    c) Not at all?
12. Is your sense of humour
    a) A bit rusty?
    b) Always in action?
    c) Non-existent?

ANSWERS

1. a. 2 b. 5 c. 0    5. a. 6 b. 3 c. 0    9. a. 4 b. 5 c. 2
2. a. 6 b. 5 c. 2    6. a. 2 b. 5 c. 4    10. a. 0 b. 6 c. 1
3. a. 5 b. 0 c. 1    7. a. 6 b. 4 c. 2    11. a. 4 b. 4 c. 2
4. a. 2 b. 6 c. 3    8. a. 6 b. 2 c. 0    12. a. 2 b. 5 c. 0

SCORES

**Over 50:** You're marvellously easy to live with, tolerant, patient, yet good company. Your partner must bless the day he/she married you!

**Between 20 and 50:** You are not difficult to live with, but a bit exasperating at times. Try seeing the other person's point of view more often.

**Below 20:** You need to watch the old selfishness and 'I'm always right' attitude!

# How Carefree Are You?

**12**

> *You may whistle a happy tune and appear to be a carefree person but honest answers to this quiz might reveal a very different side to your character... Let's find out!*

**Tick your answer to the questions, then add up the score.**

|  |  | Yes | No |
|---|---|---|---|
| 1. | Are you good at memorising telephone numbers, birthday dates, addresses? | ☐ | ☐ |
| 2. | If you were invited to go on a blind date, would you accept? | ☐ | ☐ |
| 3. | Do you often go out for a day or a weekend without planning it in advance? | ☐ | ☐ |
| 4. | If you were asked to go ski-ing, sailing, climbing or on some similar outdoor sport which you had never tried, would you agree enthusiastically? | ☐ | ☐ |
| 5. | When travelling home from work or from the shops, do you invariably go by the same route? | ☐ | ☐ |
| 6. | Do you sometimes telephone friends at the last moment and ask them over to an impromptu "surprise" party? | ☐ | ☐ |
| 7. | Do you nearly always buy the same newspapers and/or magazines? | ☐ | ☐ |
| 8. | Do you plan and arrange your holiday months in advance? | ☐ | ☐ |
| 9. | At home, do you ever get an out-of-the-blue urge to rearrange things? | ☐ | ☐ |
| 10. | When a new dance craze comes in, are you always among the first on the floor to try and master it? | ☐ | ☐ |
| 11. | Do you shop on impulse rather than by pre-arranged planning? | ☐ | ☐ |

|     |                                                                                               | Yes | No |
|-----|-----------------------------------------------------------------------------------------------|-----|----|
| 12. | Would it worry you if you had to live in a country where they speak a foreign language?      | ☐   | ☐  |
| 13. | Do you keep a day-to-day diary?                                                                | ☐   | ☐  |
| 14. | In restaurants, do you frequently order unusual and exotic dishes?                            | ☐   | ☐  |
| 15. | Do you lend money readily and not worry too much about getting it back?                       | ☐   | ☐  |
| 16. | Do you tend to sing or whistle to yourself?                                                   | ☐   | ☐  |
| 17. | Do you regard flirtations as harmless, enjoyable?                                             | ☐   | ☐  |
| 18. | If you received an invitation to a fancy dress party would you go suitable dressed?           | ☐   | ☐  |
| 19. | Are you frequently late for appointments?                                                      | ☐   | ☐  |
| 20. | To you Think it crazy to go for a moonlight swim?                                             | ☐   | ☐  |

### SCORE

| 1. Yes-0; No-1 | 2. Yes-1; No-0 |
| 3. Yes-1; No-0 | 4. Yes-1; No-0 |
| 5. Yes-0; No-1 | 6. Yes-1; No-0 |
| 7. Yes-0; No-1 | 8. Yes-0; No-1 |
| 9. Yes-1; No-0 | 10. Yes-1; No-0 |
| 11. Yes-1; No-0 | 12. Yes-0; No-1 |
| 13. Yes-0; No-1 | 14. Yes-1; No-0 |
| 15. Yes-1; No-0 | 16 Yes-1; No-0 |
| 17. Yes-1; No-0 | 18. Yes-1; No-0 |
| 19. Yes-1; No-0 | 20. Yes-0; No-1 |

### How You Rate

**18-20:** You are so carefree that you would lose your head if it wasn't part of you! You spend so much time not thinking about what you're going to do next that your life is one long muddle of missed trains, unanswered letters, forgotten birthdays and mislaid keys. You may enjoy life, but you make it difficult for others. This might be a good time to think of the people around you and show them that you're not completely scatterbrained.

**14-17:** You are light-hearted without being light-headed. You are free and easy and yet are sufficiently thoughtful and careful to make others feel at home in your presence. You do many things on the spur of the moment, but other, more important things, you organise and arrange perfectly.

**7-13:** You are a good organiser but you are not really carefree. You love planning parties, arranging holidays, but you don't enjoy the actual parties and holidays as much as you could. A little change in your life now and then would do a lot of good. Don't get too set in your ways.

**Under 7:** You really must try to relax. Stop worrying about everything—work, money, timetables, home and all the other things that go through your mind so constantly. Change your newspaper, eat somewhere different, go home another way, join a new club, try a new drink, buy some new clothes. Let things drift a bit. You'll sleep better and enjoy life more.

# How Poised Are You?

⬜ 13

> *Some of us have easy-going friendly natures, capable of getting along with people around us. A composed self-assured manner is an added attribute, bound to make one popular. So how poised are you? Discover for yourself.*

**Choose one multiple choice for each question.**
1. Do you know and admit your weak points as well as your strong ones?
   - ☐ Always
   - ☐ Occasionally
   - ☐ Seldom
   - ☐ Never
2. Do you know what social situations embarrass you and how to handle them?
   - ☐ Always
   - ☐ Occasionally
   - ☐ Seldom
   - ☐ Never
3. Can you control your emotions, such as anger and crying?
   - ☐ Always
   - ☐ Occasionally
   - ☐ Seldom
   - ☐ Never
4. When you meet a new person are your first feelings about that person judgemental or negative?
   - ☐ Always
   - ☐ Occasionally
   - ☐ Seldom
   - ☐ Never
5. Do you find humour in embarrassing situations, even when you are the one who is embarrassed?
   - ☐ Always
   - ☐ Occasionally
   - ☐ Seldom
   - ☐ Never
6. Do you know how to sit and walk with confidence?
   - ☐ Always
   - ☐ Occasionally
   - ☐ Seldom
   - ☐ Never
7. Do you handle criticism and rejection well?
   - ☐ Always
   - ☐ Occasionally
   - ☐ Seldom
   - ☐ Never
8. Is your appearance the best it can be whether on the job or just going to the store?
   - ☐ Always
   - ☐ Occasionally
   - ☐ Seldom
   - ☐ Never

9. Do you feel that your value as a person is independent of what others think of you?
   ☐ Always          ☐ Seldom
   ☐ Occasionally    ☐ Never
10. Do you hold your hands relaxed with curled fingers in a comfortable position?
    ☐ Always          ☐ Seldom
    ☐ Occasionally    ☐ Never
11. Do you feel that you have as much talent and luck as other people?
    ☐ Always          ☐ Seldom
    ☐ Occasionally    ☐ Never
12. Are your clothes comfortable and do they make you feel comfortable?
    ☐ Always          ☐ Seldom
    ☐ Occasionally    ☐ Never
13. Can you handle failure?
    ☐ Always          ☐ Seldom
    ☐ Occasionally    ☐ Never
14. Do you see good health as the basis for a good appearance?
    ☐ Always          ☐ Seldom
    ☐ Occasionally    ☐ Never
15. Do you ever compare yourself with others and feel inadequate?
    ☐ Always          ☐ Seldom
    ☐ Occasionally    ☐ Never

The old numbered questions pertain to inner poise and the even ones to visual poise. Score them separately first to see which area is most difficult for you. Then score as follows: **Always** (3 points), **Occasionally** (2 points), **Seldom** (1 point), and **Never** (0 point).

HERE'S WHAT YOUR TOTAL SCORE MEANS
**35-45 points.** You're incredible. You don't worry about poise and may have it naturally. However, some people

with no self-doubt come across as "stuck-up" or vain; so be sure to be friendly as well as poised.

**25-34 points.** Good for you! You're in there working at life and you seldom worry about poise. Use this test to find the areas you can improve and work on those.

**15-24 points.** You need improvement, but you can do it. You are in the average range where you sometimes worry, but at other times feel quite poised. Focus on the areas giving you problems and work on it.

**0-14 points.** You should definitely start working at poise. You may think about poise too much and do too little about it. Consider taking a modelling course, and do some exercising and self-evaluation to improve your appearance and self-image.

# How Cordial Are You?

**14**

> *Are you an introvert, extrovert or ambivert? Introverted people are chiefly concerned with their own problems and emotions while extroverts are interested in action, other people and being in the limelight. The ambiverts share the traits of the two, depending on their moods and the situation. This test will help you determine which type you are.*

**In each situation select the reaction that would be nearest your own.**
1. A friend invites you to join him and his friends at a picnic. When you arrive he is not there. You would
   a. Stand apart from the people and wait for him.
   b. Mingle with the group while keeping an eye out for your friend.
   c. Introduce yourself to everyone and get the picnic going.
2. A police officer is about to give you a ticket for exceeding speed limits by ten miles an hour. You would
   a. Say nothing and accept the invitation.
   b. Say you are sorry but had an urgent appointment.
   c. Tell the officer that ten miles an hour over the limit is not very important.
3. Your boss has given an order which you know will result in a loss of money to the business. You would
   a. Follow his directive.
   b. Be aware of his authority but tell him you feel he has made an unwise decision.
   c. Flatly tell him he is wrong.
4. You are entertaining a visitor who monopolises the conversation. You would
   a. Let him talk.
   b. Try to include others in the conversation.
   c. Contradict many of his statements.

5. You are asked to attend or give a talk before a school or tax-payers meeting. You would
   a. Give some excuse why you cannot attend.
   b. Prepare a speech and read it.
   c. Leap at the opportunity to express your pros or cons.

SCORING

Count the number of times you selected A, the number of times you selected B, the number of times you chose C.

In general, A-reactions indicate introverted reactions.

B is usually the choice of those who tactfully sit on the fence.

C is indicative of extroverted personalities.

ANALYSIS

**4 or more A's:** You are very likely an introverted person who tends to hide emotions, such as anger, even joys. In many incidences, you can pop out of your shell if you desire to do so.

**4 or more B's:** This is the score of those who ride with the tide. They are neither extroverted nor introverted but ambiverts who fit into situations or can take care of situations when needed.

**4 or more C's:** You are probably a highly out-going person who enjoy as being the centre of attraction. To your credit, you get things done but may walk on the toes of others in the process.

Those who score in a mixture of A's, B's and C's are usually ambiverts who react according to their own balance and mood.

# Are You Sensuous? [15]

> *Through usage the word "sensuous" has come to mean "sexy' although the dictionary definition is: "derived from or perceived by the senses." Whether we think of the word in the popular or its true meaning, some people are more sensuous than others. Like all other characteristics, this quality in one's personality makes for a richer life provided sensuousness is not allowed to rule the mind. This test asks you to check your Sensuous Rating.*

**Select the answer which fits you best.**
1. When you talk with people you usually look
   a. into their eyes.
   b. at their mouths.
   c. at their hands.
2. You have or would you like to have
   a. hair that reaches below your shoulders.
   b. short hair.
   c. several wigs of different styles and colours.
3. You use perfume or after shaving colognes
   a. regularly.
   b. never.
   c. only on evening dates or appointments.
4. If it were in your power you would sleep between
   a. unironed sheets.
   b. ironed sheets.
   c. satin sheets.
5. You prefer
   a. a brisk shower.
   b. a fast tub-bath.
   c. to lie in warm soapy bath water.
6. When you know there is a "for adults only" movie with nude scenes showing nearby, you would
   a. make an effort to see it.
   b. write it off as a waste of money and stay home.
   c. go if friends invited you.
7. You need some warm clothing. If money were no factor in your decision, you would choose
   a. a tweed jacket.
   b. a cashmere sweater.
   c. a lined denim wind-breaker.

3. When you hear a song that reminds you of a past love in your life, you usually think
   a. that music is more appealing than the mod, go-go songs.
   b. those were wonderful evenings and days.
   c. what did I ever see in him/her?
9. If you were to lose all but one of your five senses, you would wish to retain
   a. sight.
   b. the sense of smell.
   c. the ability to hear.
   d. the tactile sense (feeling).
   e. the sense of taste.
10. You are
    a. more than 10 pounds underweight.
    b. at the proper weight for height, bone-structure and age.
    c. more than 10 pounds overweight.
11. Your dancing ability is
    a. very good.
    b. good enough to get by.
    c. so poor I usually talk rather than dance.

## Scoring
1. A-5, B-10, C-3
3. A-10, B-0, C-5
5. A-5, B-0, C-10
7. A-5, B-10, C-3
9. A-3, B-0, C-3, D-10, E-5
11. A-10, B-5, C-0.

2. A-10, B-0, C-5
4. A-3, B-1, C-10
6. A-10, B-0, C-5
8. A-3, B-10, C-0
10. A-0, B-10, C-0

## Analysis
**90-110:** Both men and women in this bracket are usually sensuous personalities. There are times when they need to turn on their minds and tune out their desires to answer the cravings of their five senses. "When the cup of

any sensual pleasure is drained to the bottom, there is always poison in the dregs" (Jane Porter, English novelist).

**50-89:** This score is rated by those who often have the urge to use their senses more but for some reason are preoccupied, shy, conditioned by fear, or prudishness. All in all, it is an average score of well-adjusted teenagers and adults.

**0-49:** Those in this group tend to be desensitised. They open new vistas for themselves when they made a conscious effort to exercise their senses and to make themselves more attractive to those with whom they are in contact.

# Are You An Interesting Person?   **16**

> *The ingredients required for being "interesting" are relatively simple, if we take time to think about how we appear to others, what we have to say and the manner in which we behave with others. This test is designed to help you evaluate yourself and to give you some hints about livening up your personality.*

**Answer Yes or No.**
1. Is your conversation primarily filled with your interests, your routine, your joys and your sorrows?
 Yes____     No____
2. Do you encourage others to talk about themselves?
 Yes____     No____
3. Do you, by word and actions, show vitality?
 Yes____     No____
4. When people come to you for advice, can you help them or direct them to a source which can help?
 Yes____     No____
5. Do you have some "specialities" such as recipes, gardening techniques, mechanical improvements, or sports that you are willing to share if others are interested?
 Yes____     No____
6. Does your home contain several unusual items?
 Yes____     No____
7. Are you willing to change the subject or activity if you sense others are bored?
 Yes____     No____
8. Can you usually find some humour in most situations?
 Yes____     No____
9. When you leave home, perhaps only to go to work or shop, do you usually notice at least one thing of interest that you can share with someone else?
 Yes____     No____
10. Do you show your love and affection for others in spontaneous rather than routine ways?
 Yes____     No____

## SCORE
1. Yes-0, No-10
2. Yes-10, No-0
3. Yes-10, No-0
4. Yes-10, No-0
5. Yes-10, No-0
6. Yes-10, No-0
7. Yes-10, No-0
8. Yes-10, No-0
9. Yes-10, No-0
10. Yes-10, No-0

## YOUR SCORE

**80-100:** This score is rated by those who are usually considered to be interesting people. They listen well and may sometimes feel some of their associates are bores. They have a knack of bringing out the best in others.

**40-70:** People in this category often admit that they sometimes bore others with their own interests, such as the cute things their children say, the problems of work or long-winded showings of slides made during vacation time.

**0-30:** This low score should prompt you to change your personality from dull to bright and interesting.

# 17

## Are You A Peaceful Person?

> We are going through a period of contradictions. On the one hand there has never been such a clamour for peace; on the other, so much violence. Many "doves" are disruptive, aggressive and militant. Using strong-arm tactics they seem to say, "We will have peace if I have to kill you to get it." This test asks you to evaluate yourself carefully in order to ascertain whether or not you basically have a peaceful nature.

**Answer Yes or No.**

                                                      **Yes  No**

1. If the participants were qualified to talk about a controversial subject such as wars, sex education, drugs, I would prefer to hear a debate between two people rather than a round-table discussion. ☐ ☐
2. I usually turn off television shows which depict acts of violence. ☐ ☐
3. I like most of my family, relatives and associates. ☐ ☐
4. I believe life goes more smoothly when people pull together with a common goal in the family unit or a working situation. ☐ ☐
5. I would rather be hurt than hurt others. ☐ ☐
6. Profanity is an efficient way of venting emotions while putting one's point across. ☐ ☐
7. I always try to understand the viewpoints of others and the reasons for their actions. ☐ ☐
8. My temper is easily triggered. ☐ ☐
9. I try to get as much and no more rest and sleep than my system requires. ☐ ☐
10. I'd rather lose honestly than win dishonestly. ☐ ☐

|  | Yes | No |
|---|---|---|
| 11. I was reared in an environment that believed in western physical punishment as a disciplinary measure. | ☐ | ☐ |

### ANSWERS
1. Yes-0, No-10
2. Yes-10, No-0
3. Yes-10, No-0
4. Yes-10, No-0
5. Yes-10, No-0
6. Yes-0, No-10
7. Yes-10, No-0
8. Yes-0, No-10
9. Yes-10, No-0
10. Yes-10, No-0
11. Yes-0, No-10

### YOUR SCORE
**90-110:** Those in this bracket are peace-loving, peaceful people. They tend to mediate problems rather than to fight, to meet the opposition halfway. These are the people German poet Friedrich von Schiller had in mind when he wrote: "Peace is rarely denied to the peaceful."

**50-80:** This is a score less peaceful than that given above. Testees have learned to fight on levels such as home environment or interests in business. They talk about peace while certain things nag them. They can either "dig up the hatchet" or "hold out the olive branch."

**0-40:** People who rate this score are usually plagued by feelings of inadequacy. They have to "fight out of a hole" psychologically. And because they fear for their abilities to be peaceful with others, they will fight at the "drop of a hat." Many of these people felt that they wanted to make war in order to be killed, thus leaving the burden of their suicidal wish on someone else.

# Are You A Pushover?

**18**

> *Are you easily manipulated? Are you always doing favours that are never returned? Or are you simply very nice? Take our quiz and find out!*

**Answer the following questions as truthfully and accurately as possible. Choose one multiple choice for each question.**
1. You have saved Rs.5,000 with an eye towards some outrageously frivolous spending when the current man in your life arrives, hat in hand, begging a loan to get the sharks off his back. You
   a. Back him but only after discussing how he intends to repay you.
   b. Give him the cash. Loan sharks are serious business and there are parts of him that you would hate to see damaged.
   c. Tell him the eleventh commandment that says, "Neither a borrower nor a lender be".
2. Your friend is seeing a roaming Romeo that she hopes to tame. She hints that she wants to borrow your best string of pearls to rope him.
   a. Without waiting for her to ask, you run to your jewellery box to get the pearls and see if you have earrings and a bracelet to match.
   b. You talk about the weather.
   c. Sorry, Charlie. Since you have plans to wear it yourself tonight she is out of luck.
3. He asks you to keep a mysterious looking package. Although it is not ticking, your gut feeling tells you all is not kosher.
   a. You take the package, ask no questions and tuck it into your closet. True friends do not ask questions.
   b. Inquire about the goodies inside and take it only after you are convinced that it is safe.

c. You tell him it goes against your grain to hold mysterious packages, so how about a look-see?
4. You are working on a team project that has a tight deadline. Your co-worker must leave early (again) tonight. That leaves you stuck alone for the third time this week.
   a. What can you do? God knows, somebody has to care.
   b. You block the exit, hand her some files and pass the letters.
   c. You snitch to your supervisor. If the deadline is missed you want everybody to know it is your fault.
5. This time it is your boss who plays bad guy. You have plans to meet a friend for dinner after work, and he asks you to stay late.
   a. Batting your beautiful you explain that normally it would not be a problem but you have got special plans right after work.
   b. No way would you jeopardise your raise, so you cancel your dinner date and stay until the work is finished.
   c. Okay, you will stay, but only for an hour if your friend can make it later.
6. Your sometimes boyfriend asks you to pick up tickets for a concert he is inviting you to. As another perfect evening draws to a close he makes no move to reimburse you. So
   a. You chalk it up to the cost of a good time. Luckily payday is not far off.
   b. You wait a week and then ask him to cough up the cash or you will stop seeing him.
   c. As you leave the concert you broach the subject of accounts payable.

7. You are walking to your car at the airport when a definite executive type approaches you, holding a few coins and wearing a sorrowful expression. He tells you his wallet has been lifted and he does not have the fare to take a bus home.
   a. You empty your pocket and give him the change. Everyone knows overloaded pockets lead to holes in the lining, and it is your good coat.
   b. You play deaf, keep walking, and ignore his request.
   c. You impulsively take out Rs. 50 from your bag and tell him to take a cab. Who knows? It could happen to you.
8. Specific orders were given to the cleaners not to starch your clothes. Even so, they came back stiff enough to stand up on their own.
   a. You timidly complain before accepting the clothes the way they are.
   b. You insist loudly enough to make the manager's hair stand on end that the clothes be returned for next day service at no extra charge.
   c. Wear them the way they are, promising yourself that next time things will be different.
9. Not again! Your sister asks if you can babysit her kids for the weekend. Your plans included two days curled up with a good book and some cool lemonade. You
   a. Tell her any weekend except this one would be fine. Can she change her plans?
   b. Sure you will take them. The circus is in town.
   c. Knock the wind out of her with the news that you were planning to secretly get married that very weekend and the kids might ruin your honeymoon.

10. You and your friends go out to dinner. It has been a great evening filled with pasta, drinks and easy chatter until the bill arrives. No one makes a move. Finally you:
   a. Whip out your credit card and pay the whole bill.
   b. Take a no-nonsense approach, work out the bill including tip, and collect the money.
   c. Go hide in the ladies' room.
11. A mad dash to the grocery for a last minute container of hot fudge topping and a carton of vanilla ice cream uncovers a "buy one get one free" special on chocolates.
   a. Even though that is the last thing on your mind, you cannot resist a bargain, so you toss it into your basket anyway.
   b. You stop to take a look and wonder why anybody in their right mind would buy two jars of the stuff even if one is free.
   c. Place the cold container of ice cream on your forehead to shock your bad thoughts loose and continue to the check out counter.
12. While rummaging through a pile of vintage clothing in a crowded flea market you grab a gorgeous scarf only to discover that another bargain hunter is clutching one corner of it for dear life, too.
   a. You reluctantly let it go. Who needs the aggravation?
   b. Firmly announce you saw it first and finders keepers.
   c. Tug a little harder and may the strongest shopper win.

## SCORING

Take the following points for questions answered, and make a total.
1. a-2, b-3, c-1
2. a-3, b-2, c-1
3. a-3, b-2, c-1
4. a-3, b-1, c-2
5. a-1, b-3, c-2
6. a-3, b-2, c-1
7. a-2, b-1, c-3
8. a-2, b-1, c-3
9. a-2, b-3, c-1
10. a-3, b-2, c-1
11. a-3, b-2, c-1
12. a-3, b-1, c-2

## ANALYSIS

**25-36: Easy Mark:** Boy, can they see you coming! Unable to say "no" you are the epitome of selflessness and give of yourself freely. Born with a heart of gold, you are oblivious to the phoney-plated Philistines that prey on the pastry. Take warning—look under that rock before you place it in your garden. Soon you will learn when to play it cool so you do not get burned.

**13-24: On The Mark:** Right on target with an uncanny ability to differentiate the diamonds from the fakes, your keen sense of judgement coupled with a healthy dose of self-respect allows you to weave through shaky situations with surety. Not one to be taken advantage of easily, you can still offer help and understanding to your deserving devotees while remaining in command of your own destiny.

**Up to 12: Tough As Nails:** No one is gonna get you. No sir, no way! Secretly fuelled by the fear of being taken, you look at life with a suspicion-filled focus. Although it is wise to watch out, not every encounter has ominous undertones. Learn to relax a bit, and trust your senses. The world may seem filled with scoundrels determined to despoil you, but some of the crowd do deserve a change to prove their sincerity.

## Do You Have Charm? ⟨19⟩

> *Charm is a subtle ingredient of the personality that stems from the way people think and act. Physical attractiveness, money or expensive clothes may attract attention but, unless charm is inherent, their appeal soon vanishes.*

**Answer honestly!**
1. When you talk with a person, do you look into his/her eyes?
   Yes____   No____
2. When someone talks to you, do you give your undivided attention?
   Yes____   No____
3. Are you as polite to a waiter or sales clerk as you are to your close friends?
   Yes____   No____
4. When people, places or things please you, do you say so?
   Yes____   No____
5. Do you observe the basic rules of good grooming (clean teeth, clear breath, no body odours, neat clothing)?
   Yes____   No____
6. Is your conversation or correspondence filled with pronouns which refer to yourself (I, me, mine, my)?
   Yes____   No____
7. Do you keep your voice low and modulated while, at the same time, speak so that you can be easily understood?
   Yes____   No____
8. Do you distrust people not of your face, creed or colour?
   Yes____   No____
9. If an embarrassing situation arises for someone, do you try to draw attention away from that person rather than to prolong the mishap?
   Yes____   No____

10. Is it easy for you to smile?
    Yes____  No____
11. Do you genuinely enjoy people who are younger or older than you?
    Yes____  No____
12. Have you stopped trying to learn new things?

**ANSWERS**

| | | |
|---|---|---|
| 1. Yes-3 | 2. Yes-3 | 3. Yes-3 |
| 4. Yes-3 | 5. Yes-5 | 6. No-3 |
| 7. Yes-3 | 8. No-5 | 9. Yes-5 |
| 10. Yes-5 | 11. Yes-5 | 12. No-5. |

**YOUR SCORE**

**32-48:** People think you are a charming person. You are more concerned with others than with yourself. Doubtless you have many friends.

**20-31:** You tend to "get along" with people rather than to win them over. Take heart! Charm can be learned and practice makes it part of one's nature. If you act in an outgoing way, you, too, will be called charming.

**0-19:** This is a score which can be easily improved. Consider it as a challenge! You can be charming if you try.

## 20

## Do You Talk Too Much?

> *The Chinese philosopher, Chuang-tse, noted that "a good dog is not considered a good dog because he is a good barker. A man is not considered a good man because he is a good talker." To this, clergyman C. Simmons adds: "Great talkers are like leaky vessels; everything runs out of them." To be sure, mankind is distinguished from other animals because of his ability to communicate complex and abstract ideas in words, but the question remains: do you talk Too Much?*

**Circle the numbers which correspond to your answers.**
1. If you were to select a painting, which would you prefer?
    a. a street cafe scene     6
    b. waves breaking on rocks     3
2. How would you prefer to spend an evening?
    a. reading a book     2
    b. at a party     5
    c. at a concert     4

                                                        Yes  No

3. Do you spend much time thinking about yourself?
                                                        2   1
4. Are your memories more concerned with happy moments than with miserable happenings?
                                                        4   3
5. Do you like a certain landscape?     1    0
6. Do you wish you had more relatives?     2    1
7. Are you comfortable economically?     3    2
8. Do you wish you received more party invitations?
                                                        4   3
9. Do you watch your health?     2    1
10. Do you aim well?     0    1
11. Do you have a secret money reserve?     2    1
12. Do you know something about the care of a garden?
                                                        3   2

**SCORING**
Add the numbers which you have circled.

## ANALYSIS

**Less than 24:** You are the silent type who may tend to brood. In a way you are selfish, for others would benefit from your knowledge and opinions. Try to take an interest in the art of conversation.

**25-28:** You are likely to be a real chatterbox. Your friends and family may find it hard to follow you. Learn to listen as well as to express your own ideas and thoughts.

**29-31:** You speak when you have something worthwhile to say and you do not waste words. You give your information clearly and listen well.

**32-35:** You like to converse and exchange thoughts. However, you need the right people to stimulate you, otherwise talk becomes merely chit-chat for you. If you dislike a person, you face him or her with stony silence, but, for the most part, you are friendly and gregarious.

# Are You Young In Spirit?

**21**

> *There seems to be little relation between chronological age and one's outlook, habits, ethics—even one's physical well-being. An extraordinary person was recently encountered, jogging five miles, an exercise he took three times a week. He walked the same five miles the remaining days. This bright-eyed man had celebrated his 100th birthday yet was still vitally interested in the problems of youth, politics and world affairs. This test will help you discover if you are young in spirit.*

**Answer the following questions True or False.**
1. Hobbies may be fine for others but I am not interested.
   True____    False____
2. Even though current styles, such as mini-skirts and long hair, may not be for me, I enjoy them on the right people.
   True____    False____
3. I can name at least two modern pop singers.
   True____    False____
4. I usually enjoy talking with people who are younger than I.
   True____    False____
5. I enjoy doing things on the spur of the moment.
   True____    False____
6. Instead of doing the talking myself or listening to others, I enjoy exchanging ideas.
   True____    False____
7. Even if I am awkward, I enjoy learning current dance steps.
   True____    False____
8. In my thinking, the acquisition of money is more important than people.
   True____    False____
9. I agree with the often-used statement: "Love makes the world go 'round."
   True____    False____
10. I think the "old days" were much better than today or those days which are likely to come.
    True____    False____

11. I like to remember some of the romantic moments in my life.
   True____     False____

**Answers**
Give yourself 3 points for each of these correct answers.
| | | |
|---|---|---|
| 1. False | 2. True | 3. True |
| 4. True | 5. True | 6. True |
| 7. True | 8. False | 9. False |
| 10. False | 11. True. | |

**Your Score**

**27-33:** It is of no importance how young or old you are in terms of age. You have a youthful approach to life.

**19-26:** Testees in this range are usually youthful in their outlooks but are sometimes hemmed in by the raw feeling that life is demanding.

**0-18:** Those who rate this bracket often have lost their lust for life. New experiences, new hobbies and new adventures can give them new vistas of living.

# Are You Young At Heart?

**22**

> *We find many young people who are in the mire of mental old-age before they are 20. The secret lies in your approach to life. This test may give you some important insights.*

**Check your answers to the following questions.**
1. People younger than I am ask for my help or my advice.
   a. Never
   b. Sometimes
   c. Often
2. People in their late teens and early 20s are mature enough to have responsible positions.
   a. Never
   b. Sometimes
   c. Often
3. I try out a new dance step.
   a. Never
   b. Often
   c. Seldom
4. I'm interested in my cultural heritage.
   a. Not a bit
   b. Very much
   c. Only when it comes up
5. I read a newspaper or periodical.
   a. When I am bored
   b. With regularity
   c. Seldom
6. Fashion trends
   a. Bore me.
   b. Interest me.
   c. Are something I adopt.
7. I have
   a. One hobby.
   b. No hobby.
   c. Many hobbies.

8. Of leading pop singers, I can name
   a. Five or more.
   b. One or two.
   c. None.
9. I enjoy most
   a. Listening to others.
   b. Talking.
   c. Exchanging ideas.
10. I enjoy doing things
    a. When I am prepared.
    b. On the spur of the moment.
    c. As a matter of routine.

**ANSWERS**
Give yourself points for your answers as follows:

| | | | |
|---|---|---|---|
| 1. a-1 b-3; c-5 | | 2. a-1; b-3; c-5 | |
| 3. a-1; b-5; c-3 | | 4. a-1; b-5; c-3 | |
| 5. a-1, b-5; c-1 | | 6. a-1; b-3; c-5 | |
| 7. a-3; b-1; c-5 | | 8. a-5; b-3; c-1 | |
| 9. a-3; b-1; c-5 | | 10. a-3; b-5; c-1 | |

**YOUR SCORE**

**49-55:** This score indicates that you are youthful in spirit regardless of your age. You search, look and listen. If you put your capabilities to work for you, you will have fun all your life and never grow old at heart.

**30-48:** People in this range tend to be methodical, taking each day as it comes. It is a wholesome score. The "think young" is already a part of your personality.

**0-29:** Wake up! The world is waiting for you. Get out of the old-in-heart set, and start to live. There's plenty of time to change your outlook, but the sooner you begin to "think young" the better your life will be.

**23**

# Do You Feel Inferior?

> *Many of us harbour feelings of inadequacy. Others seek attention and sympathy by explaining in detail what sorry messes they are. Psychiatrists say that often the blustery and boastful person is, in reality, trying to hide feelings of inferiority. And the quiet little guy or gal sitting in the corner may be warm and snug with inner security. Take this quiz to help determine whether or not you nurture a sense of inferiority.*

**Choose one option from each.**
1. You are trying to solve a problem when someone silently looks over your shoulders. You would:
   a. feel jittery.
   b. be flattered.
   c. put his presence in the back of your mind.
2. When an acquaintance fails on a project, you often:
   a. are secretly pleased.
   b. try to fill the breach.
   c. worry almost as much as if it were your own error.
3. If someone makes you the brunt of a joke, you:
   a. wait for the moment when you can tell an embarrassing story about him.
   b. add to the story by making it more ludicrous.
   c. explain the serious side of the situation.
4. With an unlimited amount of money, you would:
   a. buy a few of the luxuries you have always wanted.
   b. go all out with new possessions.
   c. save it.
5. If you were invited to meet foreign royalty, you would:
   a. be pleased to have the opportunity.
   b. find an excuse for not being introduced.
   c. buy new clothing, study etiquette and nervously plan your behaviour.
6. You think that:
   a. most people are better than you.
   b. everyone has strengths and weaknesses.
   c. few have your assets and abilities.

7. If you win a trophy, you would:
   a. place it in a conspicuous place in your home.
   b. let your family or friends suggest where you should put it.
   c. tuck it away.
8. You sincerely believe:
   a. there is nothing you do really well.
   b. you do many things fairly well.
   c. you excel in one or two worthwhile skills.

**ANSWERS**
1. a-20; b-5; c-0
2. a-20; b-0; c-10
3. a-20; b-0; c-10
4. a-0; b-10; c-20
5. a-0; b-20; c-8
6. a-20; b-0; c-7
7. a-15; b-8; c-5
8. a-20; b-0; c-0

**YOUR SCORE**

**100-160 points:** You have the characteristics of a bowl of jelly. This score indicates that you punish yourself unmercifully with your feelings of inferiority. Make a list of things you can do. You will be surprised how many items you can name.

**60-99 points:** You feel secure in some of your activities—but not as much as you might be. Probably you sometimes have fearful dreams and an occasional sleepless night. Concentrate on your abilities and use them wisely.

**40-59 points:** This is a normal score. Being human and honest with yourself, you have moments when you feel inadequate. This is healthy because complete self-satisfaction stunts personal growth.

**0-39 points:** Little or no feeling of inferiority in this score. Watch out that you do not appear too cocky!

# How Tacky Are You?

**24**

> Are you tacky? Do you do tacky things, my dears?
> Well, first of all, we have to be sure what "tacky" means. The dictionary says, "shabby, dowdy, unpleasant, disagreeable, loud, tatty." It is a British expression that means "ragged and shabby".
> "Tacky" is a slang expression meaning "overdone", "in poor taste", "low standards", "poor quality" or "ignorant".
> Now that you're dying to find out your Tacky Behaviour Rating, you must take the following scientific quiz.

**Put a check mark in front of the answer that will most truthfully complete each numbered paragraph.**
1. When I'm dissatisfied with something I've bought, I
   a. Return it and get my money back.
   b. Use some of it and get my money back.
   c. Use all of it and get my money back.
2. When I picnic at a scenic viewpoint I eat lunch and
   a. Look at the scenery.
   b. Don't look.
   c. Leave garbage.
3. When I'm on the road and need a washroom, I
   a. Stop at a restaurant, order nothing and use their washroom.
   b. Order coffee in a restaurant and use their washroom.
   c. Use the bushes.
4. When grocery shopping, I
   a. Go through the checkout line politely.
   b. Hold up the line while I run back for something.
   c. Have lunch on the grapes and chocolate.
5. When I wear jewellery, I
   a. Wear ten or more pieces at one time.
   b. Wear no more than five pieces at one time.
   c. Borrow other people's.
6. When I see a newspaper at someone else's home, I
   a. Read it.
   b. Clip articles from it, without asking.
   c. Steal it.

7. When I go to a botanical garden I visit the cacti and
   a. Enjoy looking at them.
   b. Carve my name on them.
   c. Carve someone else's name on them.
8. When I play bridge, I
   a. Reassure my partner when he/she makes a mistake.
   b. Shout at my partner.
   c. Keep my bridge instruction book open on the table.
9. At a restaurant buffet I take
   a. Two helpings of food.
   b. Four helpings of food.
   c. Four helpings of food and take some home in a plastic bag.
10. When someone admires my dress, I
    a. Thank them.
    b. Tell them how old it is.
    c. Tell them how much it cost.

To get your Tacky Behaviour Rating, add up the following points for the answers you have chosen:

**ANSWERS**

| 1. a. 5 | 2. a. 5 | 3. a. 0 | 4. a. 5 | 5. a. 0 |
| b. 1 | b. 1 | b. 5 | b. 0 | b. 5 |
| c. 0 | c. 0 | c. 0 | c. 0 | c. 0 |
| 6. a. 5 | 7. a. 5 | 8. a. 5 | 9. a. 5 | 10. a 5 |
| b. 0 | b. 0 | b. 0 | b. 1 | b. 1 |
| c. 0 | c. 0 | c. 0 | c. 0 | c. 0 |

**SCORE AND RATING**

**0-16:** You may not be shabby or dowdy, but you're certainly Tacky.

**17-33:** Once in a while you do things that are in poor taste. Join the club.

**34-50:** Your score is too good to be true. Were you cheating?

## 25

## Do You Maintain Your Self-Respect?

> *The Great Greek mathematician, Pythagoras, summed up the need for self-respect when he said, "Above all things, reverence yourself." This, however, is a broad statement. Psychologists give us some key factors which lead to our being comfortable and happy with ourselves. Take this quiz to see if you are capable of maintaining your self-respect.*

**Would you answer the following questions "yes" or "no"?**

|     |                                                                                  | Yes | No |
| --- | -------------------------------------------------------------------------------- | --- | -- |
| 1.  | Do you enjoy flirtations or "affairs"?                                           | ☐   | ☐  |
| 2.  | Is your bank account often overdrawn?                                            | ☐   | ☐  |
| 3.  | Do you expect others to take care of all the chores?                             | ☐   | ☐  |
| 4.  | Is your grooming at home as good (and appropriate) as when you go out?           | ☐   | ☐  |
| 5.  | Do you consult your doctor and dentist at regular intervals?                     | ☐   | ☐  |
| 6.  | Do you usually feel proud of your accomplishments?                               | ☐   | ☐  |
| 7.  | Do you guard the health and welfare of yourself, your family and your friends?   | ☐   | ☐  |
| 8.  | Do you take care of your personal belongings?                                    | ☐   | ☐  |
| 9.  | Are you polite and kind to children?                                             | ☐   | ☐  |
| 10. | Do people, places and things genuinely interest you?                             | ☐   | ☐  |

**DESIRABLE ANSWERS**
All should be Yes *except* 1, 2 and 3.

**SCORING**
**8 to 10 correct:** You are aware of the need for self-respect and work to develop and maintain it. As Lord Alfred Tennyson, the poet, said, "Self-reverence, self-knowledge, self-control, these three alone lead life to sovereign power."

**4 to 7 correct:** Your self-respect is a little shaky. Sometimes you like yourself, but often you envy others and hate to look at yourself in your mental mirror.

**0 to 3 correct:** Start with your outward appearance because it is the thing you can see. Next, do one thing for someone else to make him or her happy. Don't be modest. Brag (to yourself) about it. Find *one* thing that you can do better than anyone else—and do it. This does not have to be something big. It could be raising radishes or collecting stamps, but you will feel a pride that obviously is underdeveloped. "One self-approving hour whole years outweigh." (Alexander Pope, English poet)

# 26

## Are You In Full Command Of Your Status Symbols?

> *As we passed over the mid-century mark, new terms came into style, one being Status Symbol, and, my dear, if you don't have some, you're just nobody—nobody at all. This quiz is designed for women.*

**Answer the following statements with a truthful Yes or No.**

|     |                                                                                                   | Yes | No |
|-----|---------------------------------------------------------------------------------------------------|-----|----|
| 1.  | Do you smile a bit pityingly at your friend's imitation jewellery and casually mention your new diamond ring? | ☐ | ☐ |
| 2.  | Have you put your poodle in a kennel because he might dirty your carpet? | ☐ | ☐ |
| 3.  | Do you order your clothes directly from the boutique? | ☐ | ☐ |
| 4.  | Do you travel abroad at least once a year? | ☐ | ☐ |
| 5.  | Does every member of your family of driving age have an automobile? | ☐ | ☐ |
| 6.  | Do you own at least two solitaire diamonds? | ☐ | ☐ |
| 7.  | Does your residence have at least two telephone numbers (preferably unlisted)? | ☐ | ☐ |
| 8.  | Have you stored your diamonds and wear only star sapphires and/or jade? | ☐ | ☐ |
| 9.  | Do you usually have your parties catered? | ☐ | ☐ |
| 10. | Can you discuss with authority your servant problems? | ☐ | ☐ |
| 11. | Are you (or will you) send your children abroad for schooling? | ☐ | ☐ |
| 12. | Do you own at least two homes for your own use? | ☐ | ☐ |

|  | Yes | No |
|---|---|---|

13. Can your husband join you any time for luncheon without checking with the boss? ☐ ☐
14. When you shop locally, do you have a special sales lady who assembles ahead of time complete outfits because she is familiar with your size, style and preferences? ☐ ☐

### ANSWERS

If you have answered **less than 3** statements with a *yes*, our hearts bleed for you. You are probably just one of those humdrum salt-of-the-earth ladies who everybody loves and who can whip up the best food in town.

**4 to 13** yes-answers prove beyond a doubt that you are Somebody. You are well informed on you status symbols and *almost* perfect in your use of them!

**14 yes**-answers is undeniable evidence that you yourself are the Symbol of the Status Symbol. Congratulations and you win the silver grey Mercedes 300!

## Can You Make Others Happy? (27)

> *It has been observed by psychologists that the happiest people are those who unstintingly and willingly give of themselves in order to make others happy. This has little to do with elaborate gifts or lavish affection. This test will give you some clues as to whether or not you make people happy.*

**A simple Yes or No would do.**
1. Is your conversation filled with negative words such as "don't," "can't," "won't?"
   Yes____    No____
2. Do you enjoy doing things for other people?
   Yes____    No____
3. Are you willing to listen to the problems of others?
   Yes____    No____
4. Do you prepare for birthdays and anniversaries with the same enthusiasm that you prepare for major holidays such as Diwali or Christmas?
   Yes____    No____
5. Do you tend to give back talk?
   Yes____    No____
6. In a quarrel, do you pursue your opinion to the bitter end?
   Yes____    No____
7. Do you believe that kindness produces kindness?
   Yes____    No____
8. Do you constantly remind people of their past mistakes?
   Yes____    No____
9. Do you downgrade others so that they lose their self-respect?
   Yes____    No____
10. Do you make it a habit to give sincere compliments when they are deserved?
    Yes____    No____
11. Can you overlook faults and accept people as they are?
    Yes____    No____

## Scoring
Give yourself 10 points for each of the following answers:

| | | |
|---|---|---|
| 1. No | 2. Yes | 3. Yes |
| 4. Yes | 5. No | 6. No |
| 7. Yes | 8. No | 9. No |
| 10. Yes | 11. Yes | |

## Your Score

**80-110:** Testees in this bracket are usually very happy people because they have learned the art of making others happy. Being able to bring happiness to others brings genuine pleasure to these people. In their case, happiness is a two-way street.

**50-70:** This is a score made often by very "practical" people who are so busy with their own endeavours that they have to think hard about making others happy. When they try to instil happiness in those around them they usually succeed.

**0-40:** Testees who rate this score are usually self-centred and insensitive to the reactions of others. They believe others should work for them rather than with them. They do not look into the eyes and hearts of others in order to give happiness.

# Do You Know The Real You? ⟨28⟩

> *Throughout the centuries, great thinkers have advised you to "know thyself"—and this means more than looking in the mirror while combing your hair. Failures in self-honesty are at the root of almost every emotional and mental disturbance. This test will give you some clues to your own ability to evaluate yourself.*

**Indicate an honest Yes or No to each question.**
1. Can you list five people who have greatly influenced you—either positively or negatively?
   Yes____            No____
2. Do you think people are frank, honest and forthright with you?
   Yes____            No____
3. Are you honest with your comments and criticisms of other people?
   Yes____            No____
4. When you are involved with other people and things go wrong, do you sincerely feel that the others are usually in error?
   Yes____            No____
5. Can you laugh at yourself?
   Yes____            No____
6. Can you list your good and bad traits, your talents and your weaknesses?
   Yes____            No____
7. Have you ever stopped to ask yourself why you are working at the job or career you now have?
   Yes____            No____
8. Do you feel all emotions can be controlled?
   Yes____            No____
9. Do you sometimes have the feeling that other people are letting you down?
   Yes____            No____
10. Do you want to become thoroughly competent, adequate, talented and intelligent in all possible ways?
    Yes____            No____

11. On the list you made for question 6, did you give more negative points than positive ones?
    Yes____   No____
12. Do weather conditions affect your moods?
    Yes____   No____
13. When invited to a party where you hardly know anyone, would you make an effort to socialise?
    Yes____   No____
14. Does the prospect of spending your birthday evening quietly at home depress you?
    Yes____   No____

ANSWERS

Give yourself 1 point for each correct answer to the following questions.

| | | |
|---|---|---|
| 1. Yes | 2. Yes | 3. Yes |
| 4. No | 5. Yes | 6. Yes |
| 7. Yes | 8. No | 9. No |
| 10. No | 11. No. | 12. Yes |
| 13. Yes | 14. Yes | |

YOUR SCORE

**0-2:** You do not see yourself as you really are: Your image is distorted like a reflection in a warped mirror in an amusement park.

**3-5:** Many of your problems stem from the fact that you either kid yourself or have not taken the time for self-evaluation. The fact, however, that you have answered some of these points correctly shows you are on the right track.

**6-8:** You dare to face yourself frankly, and from this comes a calmness and self-assurance. Experiments show that people who possess a mature knowledge of themselves suffer from less anxiety than those who lie to themselves.

**9 and above:** You have learned the secret of being true to yourself. Your reactions are mature and you can accept success and failure, love and hate without confusion or feelings of personal guilt.

## Do You Irritate Others?

**29**

> *Some people are very irritating to others but do not realise why they have this undesirable quality. Many times it stems from inferiority complexes, which they try to cover up by being critical of other people. Sometimes, too, these irritating characteristics are merely bad habits of which they are unaware. This test will help you determine if you are irritating to others.*

**Think carefully and answer the following questions honestly, with a Yes or No.**
1. Do you brag about the "big-shots" you know and/or the fabulous places you have visited?
   Yes____   No____
2. Do you often accept invitations and then turn them down at the last minute?
   Yes____   No____
3. Do you claim or hint that you have the inside dope on many things?
   Yes____   No____
4. Have you done some important things that you constantly talk about?
   Yes____   No____
5. Are you prone to correct the behaviour, language or dress of your friends?
   Yes____   No____
6. When a hostess serves you an appetizing dish, do you tell her how you make yours or how you had a superior one in a restaurant?
   Yes____   No____
7. If you buy something new, do you tell everyone how much it cost?
   Yes____   No____
8. Do you often tell others that they have aged, look tired, should see a doctor?
   Yes____   No____
9. Does it take you longer than an hour to buy a pair of shoes in your favourite store?
   Yes____   No____

10. Do you boast that you are an expert in some field—such as cuisine, fashions, sports, the arts?
    Yes____    No____
11. Is the state of your health or a previous illness or operation one of your favourite topics of conversation?
    Yes____    No____
12. Do you try to convert others to your way of life?
    Yes____    No____
13. Do you expound at length about the superior qualities of your religious or political beliefs?
    Yes____    No____
14. Is it easier for you to concoct an alibi than to admit an error?
    Yes____    No____
15. At a party are you usually the first to arrive and the last to leave?
    Yes____    No____

**ANSWERS**

**11 or more Yes answers:** You have a well-developed talent for getting on the nerves of others. People are far from joyous when they see you coming and most of your stories fall on disbelieving ears—even if they are true. These behaviour traits can be corrected if you want to and if you take the time to see yourself through the eyes of others.

**8-10 Yes answers:** You're just an average irritant and are probably saved by friends who understand and like you in spite of your scratchy characteristics.

**7 or less Yes answers:** You seldom ruffle your friends or co-workers. You give the appearance of being calm and self-assured. People like you in all probability, and you have many close friends and acquaintances. They probably come to you with their problems because they know you will not lecture, demean or flaunt your own wisdom in helping them.

# How Vulnerable Are You?

**(30)**

> This is an age of get-rich-fast and many unscrupulous people are willing to exploit the innocence or slow-wittedness of others to get ahead. In order to stay on top and avoid being victimised, one must keep one's eyes open, head clear and must possess good common sense, well-seasoned with knowledge. This test will help you evaluate if you are easily taken in.

**Answer the following questions.**
1. When a man checked out of his hotel, the bill was Rs. 300. The clerk, discovering he had charged Rs. 50 too much, sent the porter with the Rs. 50 to return to the guest. The porter, however, gave only Rs. 30 and kept Rs. 20 for himself. If the guest got a refund of Rs. 30 he paid only Rs. 270 for his room. The porter kept Rs. 20, but Rs. 270 plus Rs. 20 is Rs. 290. What happened to the remaining money?
2. A teenager told his father he was willing to mow the lawn, but brought out a chessboard with 64 squares. "When I mow it the first time," said the son, "put a penny on the first square. When I mow it the next time, double my payment. Each time double the number of pennies in the previous square."
   "Working for pennies?" laughed the father. "Sounds like an inexpensive deal to me." Was father getting a bargain?
   Yes____     No____
3. When an item is on sale which many people want, do you grab it fast?
   Yes____     No____
4. Does love tend to blind you?
   Yes____     No____
5. Are you prone to believe people because they have an honest face?
   Yes____     No____
6. Do you often go to fortune-tellers?
   Yes____     No____

7. Do you believe most of the advertising you hear or read?
   Yes____  No____
8. Are you greatly pleased when strangers say complimentary things about you?
   Yes____  No____
9. If you buy on credit, do you know the rate of interest you pay?
   Yes____  No____
10. When unsolicited merchandise is sent to you through the mails and you are later billed for it, do you pay?
    Yes____  No____

ANSWERS
1. The money is not missing. The hotel received Rs.300 less Rs. 50. This adds up to Rs. 250. The porter kept Rs. 20. The guest was given Rs. 30. This adds to Rs. 300. (20 points)
2. No. Father was not getting a bargain. By the time his son mowed the lawn 64 times, the bill would be 18, 446, 744, 073, 709, -551, 615 pennies. (20 points)
3. No
4. No
5. No
6. No
7. No
8. No
9. Yes
10. No. 10 points each.

YOUR SCORE
**90-120:** Testees in this range are sometimes but not often "taken in". They tend to be those who would not take a wooden nickel and who evaluate carefully. They study

every aspect of buying, compare costs and are aware that the hand is quicker than the eye.

**50-80:** Testees in this range often tend to complain that they have been victimised by others. Tests such as this have, in many cases, alerted them to the cautions of hidden costs, the high price of judging one on his face value.

**0-40:** Testees in this range are easy victims of scalpers.

# Are You Stubborn?

**31**

> *Dr. A.A. Brill, world-famous psychoanalyst, once said: "Be careful not to confuse determination with stubbornness. A little determination is fine, but too much is no good." The following quiz will help to determine how stubborn you are.*

**Answer Yes or No.**

                                                           Yes  No

1. Do you feel your parents exerted domineering discipline over you during your childhood and youth? ☐ ☐
2. Do you like strong bright colours for your clothing? ☐ ☐
3. Do you tend to hold to your own opinion against contrary evidence? ☐ ☐
4. Do you read on an average of at least half an hour each day? ☐ ☐
5. Do you consistently read the same newspaper and magazines? ☐ ☐
6. Do you (or would you) always vote a straight party ticket regardless of the qualifications of the candidate? ☐ ☐
7. Can you usually follow the argument of another person, even if you do not agree with his or her opinions? ☐ ☐
8. Would you shove rather than let anyone crowd into a line ahead of you? ☐ ☐
9. Is your handwriting broad and heavy? ☐ ☐
10. Do you think every section of the nation has some advantages, beauties, and good things to be said for it? ☐ ☐
11. If someone disagrees with you, do you speak more loudly? ☐ ☐
12. Have you completed (or plan to) at least a high school education? ☐ ☐
13. Do you enjoy jokes which belittle and/or ridicule the opposite sex? ☐ ☐

|  | Yes | No |
|---|---|---|
| 14. Do you usually obey signs, such as "Private Road," "No U-turn," "No Smoking," "Exit Only?" | ☐ | ☐ |
| 15. Do you hesitate to try new foods? | ☐ | ☐ |
| 16. Do you openly (or secretly) distrust foreigners? | ☐ | ☐ |
| 17. Is it difficult for you to admit you are wrong? | ☐ | ☐ |
| 18. Do you become angry if you cannot have your own way? | ☐ | ☐ |
| 19. Are you your own best doctor? | ☐ | ☐ |
| 20. Do you talk more than you listen? | ☐ | ☐ |

Check the answers below with your answers and give yourself one point for each correct one. After you add up your points, see the paragraph relating to your total score.

| | | |
|---|---|---|
| 1-No | 2-No | 3-No |
| 4-Yes | 5-No | 6-No |
| 7-yes | 8-No | 9-No |
| 10-Yes | 11-No | 12-Yes |
| 13-No | 14-Yes | 15-No |
| 16-No | 17-No | 18-No |
| 19-No | 20-No. | |

**Your Score**

**16-20:** You are motivated by a highly flexible attitude. Very likely your friends think of you as a "middle-of-the-roader." You will have to answer for yourself whether or not you are a pawn who can be pushed around.

**10-15:** Determination is a large part of your makeup.

Your actions are strongly set and people know they have to be equally forceful and logical in dealing with you.

**6-9:** You are ruled by a "made-up mind" and are often blinded by many of your own ideas.

Take advantage of any communication with other people.

If you read and listen, you are bound to find some values other than your own rather self-centred opinions.

**0-5:** You have heard that statement "stubborn as a mule" and, unfortunately, you fall into this category whether you realise it or not.

It is likely that people have learned to live "around" you rather than "with" you. Very probably you have many admirable traits, but flexibility and open-mindedness are not among them.

With this score, you will probably throw the paper down and shout, "The test is wrong. I am not stubborn! I'm not! I'm not!"

# How Imaginative Are You?

**32**

> *It is hard for us to imagine, in this modern age, that there are still primitive tribes of people on earth who have not imagined the use of the wheel, which we take for granted. This test will help you evaluate your own powers of imagination.*

**Choose what you consider correct from the following questions.**
1. When you are about to fall asleep, do you often find yourself reviewing the day's activities?
   Yes____  Sometimes____  Never____
2. When you awaken from a night's sleep, do you find yourself suspended between a dream and reality for some time?
   Yes____  Sometimes____  Never____
3. Have you ever tried to write a novel, a short story, or poetry?
   Yes____  No____
4. When surrounded by a group of strangers, as on a train or in a restaurant, do you find it interesting to imagine the lives of those around you?
   Yes____  Sometimes____  Never____
5. Are forms and colour especially important to you?
   Yes____  No____
6. When you read a novel or short story, do you simultaneously envision the people and places in detail?
   Yes____  Sometimes____  Never____
7. Do you think that if you were to overcome certain personality problems your life would be more successful?
   Yes____  No____
8. Do you find yourself upset for no reason?
   Yes____  Sometimes____  Never____
9. Do you enjoy reading stories which involve the supernatural or science-fiction?
   Yes____  Sometimes____  Never____

10. When you are narrating a story, do you visualise yourself in each character's role?
    Yes____    No____
11. When you see a movie, do you put yourself into the scenes, or put yourself in the role of an actor or actress?
    Yes____    Sometimes____    No____
12. Do certain odours bring back some childhood or teenage memories?
    Yes____    Sometimes____    No____
13. While planning a holiday do you visualise the place as described in a tourist brochure?
    Yes____    Sometimes____    No____

## Scoring
1. Yes-0; Sometimes-1; Never-5
2. Yes-5; Sometimes-3; Never-0
3. Yes-5; No-0
4. Yes-5; Sometimes-3; Never-0
5. Yes-5; No-0
6. Yes-5; Sometimes-2; Never-0
7. Yes-5; No-0
8. Yes-0; Sometimes-5; Never-0
9. Yes-5; Sometimes-5; Never-0
10. Yes-5; No-0
11. Yes-5; Sometimes-5; No-0
12. Yes-5; Sometimes-5; No-0
13. Yes-4; Sometimes-5; No-0

## Analysis
**45 or more:** People who rate this score have keen, imaginative minds. This very fact, however, may lead them to live in a "dream world' and to escape from everyday realities.

**25-44:** This is a healthy, normal score, blending practicality with imagination.

**0-24:** This is a poor measurement for imagination. The enjoyment and productivity of your imagination can be increased by consciously trying.

# ㉝ Do You Try Too Hard To Be Popular?

> *Many wise men and women have made comments about the desire to be popular. It is human nature to want to be liked, accepted—yes, even to be popular—but many of us work so hard, reach out so far to be admired that we defeat our own purpose. This test will help you assess whether or not you are striving too hard to be accepted or if you are on the right road to becoming more popular.*

**Select the reaction which is nearest your own to each of the following situations.**
1. Someone important person tells a joke which is offensive to you. You would
   a. Laugh because everyone else is laughing?
   b. Flatly state you did not approve of the joke?
   c. Smile politely and pretend you didn't get the full impact?
2. On the job your superior "rubs you the wrong way." Psychologically speaking, there is a personality conflict. You would
   a. Cover your feelings by being especially nice to this person?
   b. Shun the person as much as possible?
   c. Go about your tasks as efficiently as possible?
3. You suddenly find that you have some extra money. You would
   a. Buy food and drinks for everyone you meet?
   b. Stash it away for a rainy day?
   c. Plan special gifts or treats for a few special friends?
4. On special occasions, such as holidays and birthdays, do you
   a. Usually send more cards and messages than you receive?
   b. Seldom or never send cards?
   c. Send about as many as you receive?

5. You are urged to participate in experiments with drugs. The rest of your crowd are in favour but you are reluctant. You would
   a. Accept the invitation?
   b. Refuse to associate with any member of the group again?
   c. Refuse but continue your associations as if nothing had occurred?
6. How often do you take offence at what people say or do?
   a. Never?
   b. Often and you let the offender know it?
   c. Occasionally, depending on what is said or done?
7. During a conversation, you refuse to listen to other people, but turn the stream of conversation to matters which concern you. How often is this?
   a. Never
   b. Sometimes
   c. Always

### Scoring
Give yourself 3 points for each A answer, 1 point for each B answer, 2 points for each C answer.

### Your Score
**15-21:** Those who rate in this bracket often sacrifice their own personalities in an effort to be accepted. They sometimes break their own moral and ethical codes in order to be "one of the gang".

**10-14:** This is a score rated by those who usually abide by their own convictions but are willing to let others have theirs. They are accepted because of both characteristics.

**6-9:** This low score usually is made by those who do not care whether or not they are accepted or popular. In some cases, testees in the bracket seem to take a certain pride in being disliked.